FOUR KEYS OF THE KINGDOM

How Israel, Identity, Intimacy, and Industry Come Together for Living a Kingdom Life

JEDEDIAH AND TIFFANY DRENTH

ISBN 979-8-89043-142-4 (paperback)
ISBN 979-8-89043-143-1 (digital)

Christian Faith Publishing
832 Park Avenue
Meadville, PA 16335
www.christianfaithpublishing.com

Printed in the United States of America

CONTENTS

Introduction..v

Israel 1

Identity 12

Intimacy...29

Industry 38

Concluding Thoughts 45

INTRODUCTION

This book is for all the faithful ones in Jesus, who although they study the Bible, seek holiness, and desire new life, still feel bound by the shackles of past mistakes, present problems, and future fears. It is also for new believers in Jesus and for those curious about Jesus. No matter what category you identify with, our goal is to lead you in discovering how in Jesus, there really is *new* life available to *you*. Far too often, our Christian lives are bound by small thinking, weak faith, and low expectancy. Frustration often follows when things don't turn out right, and we turn against God in our disappointment. The truths in this book will probably offend you. They offended us when we first began to learn and apply them in our own lives. However, if you're willing to push past the offense, you will find that the Lord has freedom, peace, and abundant life for you on the other side. The things that have held you back will lose their grip and you will be free indeed!

> So if the Son sets you free, you are truly free.
> (John 8:36 NLT)

The Bible teaches us that Jesus loves everyone, and He desires that all would be saved and set free. The phrase "Jesus loves you" is more than a kitschy slogan on a church sign. It's the beginning and end of who you are and where you are going.

When Jesus stated that the "Kingdom of Heaven is at hand,"[1] He wasn't just blowing smoke! He was announcing that His kingdom's culture was about to impact the earth like never before. It did, and this book is an invitation for you to rethink what it means to live in His kingdom's culture. You will find that you are connected to a far greater story than your circumstances might indicate and that you are connected to an ancient love story which began in the Garden of Eden and is still playing out in front of you. This story sets the stage for your redemption. When Jesus taught the disciples to pray, He prayed, "Your kingdom come, Your will be done, on earth as it is in Heaven."[2] In this prayer, Jesus indicates how God's desire is that His will and His way of living would manifest itself on earth. We call this will and way of living the kingdom of heaven. God's way of accomplishing this is through us. Our task is then to live our lives on earth in such a way that the culture of heaven manifests itself on the earth through us. This is our goal. We have discovered that unlocking a kingdom of heaven lifestyle, or a *kingdom life* as we call it, begins by understanding where we came from. To properly understand where we came from, we must learn the significance of Israel, the truth of our God-given identities, the beauty of intimacy with God, and the impact of industry.

[1] Matthew 10:7
[2] Matthew 6:10

ISRAEL

Hear, O Israel: The LORD our God, the LORD is one.
—Deuteronomy 6:4 (NIV)

The Good News

Christians talk about the good news of the Gospel, but if the majority of people were honest, it hasn't felt like good news at all. It has felt like a list of rules. It has felt like a disappointment. This is because their experience with God hasn't lived up to their expectations. For others, it has looked like a lot of pain inflicted by the church. The church is made up of people who have been hurt by the brokenness in our world, and we know from experience that hurt people hurt people. We expect better from the church, and rightfully so, but unfortunately the church is far from looking like the pure and spotless bride that Jesus talks about it being. If you have ever heard an evangelist speak, it is likely that you have heard a compelling conversion story where someone's life was radically changed by Jesus. It is wonderful to celebrate such victories, and we ask for more like them, but how often does the celebration turn to questioning? This questioning might start with feeling a twinge of guilt for not being as passionate about the Gospel as the radical convert. Soon, you are caught up in self-condemnation, or perhaps you have inadvertently placed God on trial and are condemning Him for not moving powerfully in your own life.

How many times have you tried to do the right things, yet the results don't seem to be working like you expected? The devil doesn't mind when you try to affect change in your life by your own strength or by the strength of religion. He knows it will likely exhaust you and lead to your giving up. The best way to effect positive change in your life is to replace lies with truth. The devil is a liar, and his weapon is deception. So if you know the truth, you will not get bludgeoned by his lies. Being honest (truthful) before God is one of the best places to start the process of getting past feeling stuck. The Lord wants your heart; He wants your whole heart. This includes the parts of your heart that you aren't sure if you want more of God in them yet. Our hope as you read this is that you will determine in your heart to risk trusting God's truth at new levels, even when your perceived reality doesn't seem to agree with what He says. His love and truth go hand in hand. It might feel too risky, but you must believe that God loves you more intimately, more perfectly, and more completely than any spouse, friend, parent, or child ever has. His love isn't contaminated by selfishness or deception, so His love is absolutely trustworthy.

As you look at the first key of the kingdom, understanding Israel, we encourage you to do this: open your heart to the possibility that ever since the beginning of time, God has desired communion with His people. We are not talking about the sacrament of communion; we are declaring that God has always wanted to share life with you! He desires to be in fellowship with you and to participate in life with you. God didn't suddenly become love when He decided to send Jesus into the world. He has been working to captivate the hearts of His people ever since Genesis. Ephesians 1:4–5 tells us that God "chose us in Him before the foundation of the world" and that He "destined us in love" to be His children (TPT).

John 13:1 (TPT) tells us,

> Jesus knew that the night before Passover would be his last night on earth before leaving this world to return to the Father's side. All throughout His time with his disciples Jesus had demonstrated

a deep and tender love for them. And now He
longed to show them the full measure of his love.

God has been lovingly pursuing us, His created people, even before mankind sinned in the Garden of Eden. Jesus's quest on earth was a culminating expression of God's love toward us. Learning about God's relationship with Israel is an important foundation for understanding God's relationship with you. Jesus was born as an Israelite, and most details of His coming were foretold through the Israelites. The Bible teaches that He came first to his own people, and then extended His gift of redemption to all people. Since Israel has a long history of being in a relationship with God, it is helpful to learn from their experience of living in a relationship with God. Although this section can be heavy, we encourage you to look at these familiar truths with an open heart and allow the Holy Spirit to illuminate Himself to you at a greater level.

The Gospel in Genesis

> Then the man and his wife heard the sound of
> the Lord God as he was walking in the garden in
> the cool of the day. (Genesis 3:8 NIV)

Before sin entered the world, Adam and Eve walked with God in the cool of the day. Take a moment to imagine a relationship and conversation with a friend on an evening walk, the kind of relationship where you share highlights from your day and the thoughts dominating your mind, a relationship free of judgment, tension, or pain. Wouldn't that have been incredible to participate in? Unfortunately sin entered the world, severing the friendship between God and humankind—the worst divorce in history. The man and woman who were created to have a relationship with God could no longer enjoy Him because of their sins. They were cast out of the Garden of Eden. A cherubim with a flaming sword blocked access to the Tree of Life.[3] Adam and Eve had to be prevented from eating from the Tree of Life in their sinful state. If they had eaten of it, they would have been stuck in their guilty state forever. So even in the seeming rejection of humankind by banishing them from the Garden, it was actually God's goodness at work. God loved His people enough to protect them from being stuck in a separated state forever. Our all-knowing God had a plan to restore humankind back to their original identity.

To understand the restoration of our souls, we need to recognize the magnitude of separation that sin causes. We serve the Holy God. His holiness is so pure, so perfect, and so beautiful that sin can have no part in it. This means that when we are ruled by sin, we cannot be ruled by God. If our primary relationship is with sin, our primary relationship cannot be with God. This would be bad news for us, who were born into the rule of sin if there was no way to escape the rule of sin. However, Jesus came and took our place by taking on the sin of the world and suffering the just consequence for that sin. In doing so, God now offers *Jesus's* perfection, to be *our* perfection. He took on our sins, so we could take on His perfection! God's perfection pushed us out of His presence when we were in sin, but now His perfection draws us into His holy presence. God's perfection once kept us from glory, but now it's because of His perfection that we have hope of future glory. We wouldn't want heaven to be tainted by sin, and it most certainly would be if it was full of sinful people! Isn't it good that God isn't okay with sin? Isn't it even more wonderful that He made a way for our sins to be removed so that we can access Him in His perfection? He is the perfect Father, and through Jesus's sacrifice, we can have Him as our perfect Father! We now have total access to a perfect friend. The world, in all its attempts, hasn't offered us anything perfect, but God has.

---

[3] Genesis 3:24

The Nation of Israel

Throughout history, there has never been a nation more controversial in geopolitical and religious conversations than Israel. From wars, exile, pilgrimage, and success, the nation of Israel and the Jewish people have faced some of history's greatest tragedies and triumphs. Today, Israel is still a hot-button issue in both the religious and secular worlds. Many Western Christians are confused as to why this seemingly obscure nation in the Middle East is relevant to their faith apart from the Old Testament. However, as you read the Bible, it is difficult to ignore the continual hand of God on the nation of Israel and the Jewish people. It is clear that from Genesis to Revelation, Israel was, and still is God's chosen people. Understanding God's intimate involvement with Israel is essential for laying the foundation for our Christian faith. As Christians, we have called on the Jew named Yeshua (Jesus) to be our Savior. It is only fitting that we learn how to identify with the nation and people that we have been grafted into.

The Framework of Sacrifice

The sacrificial systems in the Torah (Genesis, Exodus, Leviticus, Numbers, and Deuteronomy) were put into place to atone for sin. It laid out the requirements for the Jewish people to right themselves in the eyes of God. It is through this framework that we come to understand the cross of Christ. The Bible tells us,

> For the wages of sin is death, but the gift of God
> is eternal life in Christ Jesus our Lord.[4]

We have already discussed how sin separates us from the Holy God. This verse tells us that death is the result (or wage) of sin. According to the Torah, sin had to be atoned for through the sacrifice of animals. Even with this shedding of blood, the Israelites

---

[4]   Romans 6:23

were still unable to enter the presence of their holy God. The priests were the only people allowed to minister before God, and only one priest a year was selected to enter the presence of God in the innermost portion of the temple, the Holy of holies.[5] If these sacrifices couldn't restore the Israelites to their original intent, then what did they accomplish? The Old Testament sacrifices allowed the Israelites to prioritize a relationship with God. They offered a temporary covering for their sin that pointed to the future and final covering provided by Jesus's crucifixion. This shedding of blood led the way for the sacrificial Lamb of God to be our perfect redemption.

If you grew up in a church, this might feel familiar or perhaps like old news. Our request is that you allow this *old news* to be fresh in your mind so that Jesus's accomplishments in coming to earth will permeate your soul, mind, and spirit. Jesus's death on the cross and the shedding of His blood accomplished what the Levitical sacrifices could not. He effectively redeemed the Jewish people from continually offering temporary sacrifices. These sacrifices had to be done annually at appointed times in addition to any time a sin was committed. As Christians, we call on the perfect Lamb of God who took away this need to continually offer sacrifices. Jesus became our *once-and-for-all sacrifice*. In addition to saving the Jews from this system, Jesus settled the debts owed by all people for their sins so that those who would call on His name and identify with His sacrifice for them would be restored to their original God-ordained identities. Now let's return to the Garden of Eden.

New Fulfilling the Old

Many Christians in the western church claim that since we are in the new covenant of Jesus's blood, the Jewish roots of Christianity are no longer relevant. There is another group of Christians who emphasize keeping the commands found in the old covenant, such as keeping a kosher diet and practicing Jewish festivals. Both groups have points worth considering. The point that we would like to make

---

[5]   Hebrews 9:7

is that the Old Testament and the New Testament are not in opposition to each other. Understanding that the new covenant is the fulfillment of the old covenant allows us to retain the fullness of what both communicate. People like to split the Old Testament and the New Testament and frequently equate them with the old covenant and the new covenant. The reality is that the Old Testament contains numerous prophecies, types, and shadows that foretell the coming of the new covenant. The New Testament gospels begin under the old covenant and continue to remain under that covenant until the resurrection and ascension of Jesus. When asked what the biggest difference between the Old Testament and the New Testament is, many would claim the old covenant and the new covenant. The reality is that the biggest difference is simply the page between the two. God is the same yesterday, today, and forever.[6] If He doesn't change, how could His love story to His people change?

Types and Shadows of God's Redemption

The bondage of the Jewish people (or Hebrew people as they were known at the time) in Egypt under a harsh Pharaoh is a picture of our bondage to sin. Moses, a Hebrew by birth, was a picture of Christ the Redeemer. He was raised as a prince but willingly gave up his life of royalty to identify with the enslaved Hebrew people. Furthermore, he later laid down his quiet life as a shepherd and chose to follow God's call to lead Israel out of slavery.

In the record of Exodus, we learn how the angel of death was coming to take the firstborn male of every family as the last of ten plagues brought against the Egyptians. The people were instructed by God, through Moses, to apply the blood of a lamb on their doorposts. This was done on the evening before the plague came. This blood from the sacrificed lambs would communicate to the angel of death to pass over the covered home. This shed blood was also necessary to make it to the crossing of the Red Sea. This is a depiction of Christ's death on the cross making a way for us to pass through the

---

[6] Hebrews 13:8

impossible. It is this application of blood from a sacrifice that made leaving slavery and entering the promised land possible. The same principle is true for us today. Just as the Hebrew people could not access the promised land by staying in Egypt, we cannot enter our promised land if we continue living in the slavery of sin. When we first discovered the shadows of Christ in the Passover account found in Exodus, we saw that the Old Testament scriptures were full of accounts that proclaimed the coming of King Jesus.

The story of Moses and the Exodus from Egypt is surely a compelling prophetic picture, but the Old Testament has other accounts that point to God's heart for redemption and the coming Messiah too. When we look at the account of Noah, we see that he followed God by building a massive ship in a day when ships weren't a thing. By doing so, he served as a redeemer for all humankind and all land-dwelling creatures. Joseph heeded the Lord's instructions regarding the coming seven years of plenty that would be followed by seven years of famine which came through Pharaoh's dreams. He served as a redeemer to both Israel and Egypt, saving them from famine. Esther recognized her favorable position and was willing to go before the king to stand in the gap for the Israelites and served as a redeemer. King David fought many battles to protect the sovereignty of Israel, again serving as a redeemer. All these people were prophetically forecasting the coming Messiah. They were revealing something about God's heart for His people. We see in these events how God loves His people, wants to save His people, and has been calling His people back to Himself since their sin forced them out of the Garden.

The Jews' Rejection of Jesus

We see that God was orchestrating a grand narrative to prepare the way for the coming King. However, when Jesus, the High King of heaven, came to earth to redeem His people, the Jewish people missed Him. They missed their redemption by clinging to the proverbial bondage of Egypt. In their case, it wasn't slavery in Egypt, but it was an enslaving religious spirit that had associated itself with the Torah. This time, the slave master actually claimed to be God's Levitical law so that the people trapped in it were deceived into thinking they were doing the will of God. They had lost their relationship with God and had attached themselves to human interpretations of what God had said. The devil is a liar!

Now before scoffing at the Jewish people for missing their true King, it is important to ask God to show you if you are deceived into believing lies about who God is and how you relate to Him. We can also recognize how in their refusal to receive King Jesus, Gentiles (the non-Jewish people) have an opportunity to call on Christ and be saved.

Gentiles Welcomed In

> Did God's people stumble and fall beyond recovery? Of course not! They were disobedient, so God made salvation available to the Gentiles. But he wanted his own people to become jealous and claim it for themselves. Now if the Gentiles were enriched because the people of Israel turned down God's offer of salvation, think how much greater a blessing the world will share when they finally accept it. I am saying all this especially for you Gentiles. God has appointed me as the apostle to the Gentiles. I stress this, for I want somehow to make the people of Israel jealous of what you Gentiles have, so I might save some of them. For since their rejection meant that God offered salvation to the rest of the world, their acceptance will be even more wonderful. It will be life for those who were dead!" (Romans 11:11–15 NLT).

Now we can see from these New Testament passages and Old Testament accounts that the God of all the earth has been wooing, calling, and paving the way for His chosen people Israel since the beginning. This does not lessen the inclusion of the Gentiles, but it is imperative that Gentiles recognize that while God's redemption through faith is for them as individuals, it is also another avenue for God to provoke jealousy in the Jews so that they might be drawn toward God as His goodness is displayed in the lives of those who trust in Jesus. Because true life in Jesus results in a genuinely attractive, free, significant, and favored life, it should cause the lost to not only be curious but to flock to the gospel of Jesus in droves with eager hearts.

Aligning Your Heart with God's Heart for Israel

If we have truly made Jesus our Lord and Savior, then we have the privilege and duty to align our desires with His. It is now imperative that we join King Jesus in blessing Israel and longing for their return to Him! The Lord's eye remains on them so our eyes should also be fixed on them with eager anticipation for their redemption.[7] A helpful step in aligning our hearts with His regarding people and nations is to recognize that a biblical worldview reveals only two groups of people in the world: Jews and Gentiles. Simply put, Jews are the descendants of Abraham, Isaac, and Jacob, and they are commonly referred to as the chosen people of God. Gentiles make up the remainder of people and were not part of God's elect until Jesus.

It is through Jesus that we who fall under the Gentile category have been grafted into the Jewish blessing and favor of God. The Bible is clear that God still desires that His people, the Jews, would come to know Jesus, their redeemer. Therefore, we must bless Israel.[8] We must stand for Israel, pray for Israel, and identify with Israel. This is not a political statement, although it has geopolitical implications. It is a biblical perspective. It is the perspective that God commands His followers to adhere to. Much of Western Christendom has disregarded the call to bless and stand with Israel. However, as we have seen from the biblical account, the Jewish people are central to the history of God interacting with humankind. Does it not follow

---

[7] Numbers 24:9
[8] Genesis 12:3

that they must also be central to the Christian's story? Jesus was fully Jewish—that alone should compel us to honor them.

This brief overview of Jewish history provides a better understanding of where Jesus came from. We are also better able to understand the necessity of His sacrifice on the cross. By grasping more of what was accomplished on the cross, our new identity as the redeemed takes on more value. We have unveiled the first key to living a kingdom life, the significance of Israel to the Christian faith.

IDENTITY

People are searching to discover who they are. The world is flying apart all around us, and many people grow up without ever discovering their true identities. Secular leaders are telling them to find their identities through introspection, exploration, and self-discovery. All the while, they are feeding them lies about how to dress, behave, view others, eat, and what to do with their emotions and resources. The Western church, in contrast, tells them that they can find their true identities through the church, yet this doesn't seem to be working either. People are leaving the church at the highest rate this nation has seen.[9] It would seem that neither option is correct because so many people in both camps are still searching for identity. There is an expectation that people in the church should have secure identities *in Jesus*, with which we would agree. The problem lies in that the people recommending this are saying it because it is true and not so much that they have actually experienced it for themselves. Too often, they come up with a complex course and lead people through it. Once through the complicated path, they are left feeling more drained because their *freedom* is achieved through more works rather than the freedom offered in their God-given identities. When freedom is dependent on works, people will eventually fail. This failure births shame.

[9] In 2019, David Kinnaman, Barna president and author of *Faith for Exiles: 5 Ways for a New Generation to Follow Jesus in Digital Babylon*, revealed that 64 percent of people (ages eighteen to nineteen years old) with Christian backgrounds left the church.

Revealing Shame

When a person fails to live how they ought to, the devil uses it as an opportunity to introduce shame. Thoughts are planted to deceive the well-meaning Christian into thinking they really are a disgrace to Jesus and are not worthy of bearing His name. Fortunately, God looks at those who are redeemed *through* Jesus and *His* righteousness. If they don't combat the lies with God's truth that they are free, made whole, forgiven, and filled with God's glory, then they will likely attempt to cover that shame. The fear that others will see the ugliness trapped inside causes them to desperately find ways to control their environments.

Failure to succeed at control causes more shame. Failure is usually accompanied by shame and just as a three-stranded cord is much more difficult to break than a single strand, this cycle of shame, fear, and control can be very difficult to break out of.[10] People usually try even harder to control by pretending to be living in the freedom offered. This is not freedom. While many try to control or hide their shame, there is a trend with another group to continually celebrate their shortcomings to *be real*. This is nothing short of giving glory to the devil. Both of these abysmal paths will lead you down the rabbit hole of self-consciousness. Introspection and self-discovery can lead to self-consciousness and self-centeredness if they result in a preoccupation with self. The devil loves to keep your focus on yourself because he knows you are incapable of saving yourself. So how do we escape this identity crisis? Is it even possible?

Your Identity in Him

The way of escape is really quite simple. It takes work and effort, but the process is not complicated. If you want to live in freedom, you have to look at yourself through Jesus who saved you. It's only

______

[10] The Shame-Fear-Control Cycle was first presented to us through Restoring the Foundations International ministries. For more information on this topic, please visit restoringthefoundations.org.

through seeing yourself in light of the effectiveness and sufficiency of the cross that you can rightly judge yourself. When God looks at you, He sees what Jesus paid for—the purified you. He now sees you as His holy, spotless son or daughter. This isn't just a nice thing to say! This is your real identity now. But it's on you to decide if you'll believe it or not. The more you *choose* to believe this, the more you will be set free. 1 Peter 2:9–10 (NIV) says:

> But you are a chosen people, a royal priesthood, a holy nation, God's special possession, that you may declare the praises of him who called you out of darkness into his wonderful light. Once you were not a people, but now you are the people of God; once you had not received mercy, but now you have received mercy.

So what happens when you sin? Does that tarnish your purity before God? The Bible states that you are saved through faith, not good works. Romans 5:2 (TPT) reads,

> Our faith guarantees us permanent access into this marvelous kindness that has given us a perfect relationship with God.

However, sin gives rights to the devil, who opposes God, to wreak havoc in your life. Romans 6:16 (TPT) says:

> Don't you realize that grace frees you to choose your own master? But choose carefully, for you surrender yourself to become a servant—bound to the one you choose to obey. If you choose to love sin, it will become your master, and it will own you and reward you with death. But if you choose to love and obey God, he will lead you into perfect righteousness.

It is clear that God wants His people to "go and sin no more."[11] However, if we do sin, then we can approach the throne room of God through Jesus our intercessor. It is through Him that we can ask for and receive forgiveness. From there, we get to move on in our restored purity.

It might also be helpful to clarify something that is often miscommunicated. We grew up hearing people say that "Jesus just came to redeem a sinner like me." This is simply not true! God did not come to redeem sinners. He came to redeem his lost sons and daughters! Our original created identity was to be His children. Let us say this again: We were created with the intent to be God's children. The Bible teaches us that God made mankind in *His image*.[12] Mankind was not made in the image of *a sinner*. It is true that we were born into sin and that caused separation from God, but His purpose in redeeming us wasn't to *change* our created intent. It was to *restore* us to our created intent.

Dualism

Dualism is the idea that we have to live in a constant battle between a sin nature and righteous nature. It is a cancer in the church that has invaded many well-meaning believers. Teaching a dual nature is not a benign disagreement of theological interpretation. It is debilitating. Dualism at its core teaches that we do not have victory over sin. It convinces its followers to put off the victory won by Jesus on the cross until we arrive in heaven. The effects are that many of Jesus's followers submit to sin ruling their lives. Do you remember what Romans 6:16 says about this? Do you want sin to be your master?

Dualism prevents the redeemed from stepping into their full power and authority in the here and now. It also cripples people by leading them to believe they cannot withstand the temptation to do shameful things. Proclaiming dualism and our ineptitude to have victory over sin is synonymous with scorning the cross of Christ. It

---

[11] John 8:11
[12] Genesis 1:27

implies at its core that the cross was not sufficient to save us from sin. It is demonic in origin. Where does God say in the Bible to have two minds? Isn't this the result of demons? Having multiple voices telling us things that are contrary to the truth was not what Jesus came to give us. Truth is singular. God is the source of truth, and He doesn't contradict Himself with differing opinions or impossible yokes. Why would we, as His image bearers, do the opposite? We cannot believe that we are made new in Christ *and* believe that our old sin-ruled self hasn't been conquered. If we teach that the Gospel was insufficient to do what it set out to do, then our entire Gospel is a lie! But thank God that this is not the truth! We have been set free and made new in Christ.

Before we go any further, let's address the question that undoubtedly follows the above statements: "If I still sin, or struggle with x, y, or z, then how am I not still a sinner?" We know this attitude because we carried it for a long time. We wanted to believe that the Gospel actually could set us free from habits or hurts that we couldn't seem to shake, but as hard as we would try to change, the change did not come. Frustration did, along with shame, fear, and control. Continually dwelling on the areas of our lives that were falling short did not bring freedom. Focusing on a recurrent sin with the goal of eradicating it never actually brought freedom from that sin. It was when we truly repented and began declaring the truth of our identity that is found in the Bible over our experiences that we started to get the breakthrough we were desperately longing for. Romans 1:6 reads,

> In Jesus Christ you individually discover who you are. (*Mirror Bible*[13])

We are convinced that if you want to live in the freedom promised in the Bible, then you need to determine in your heart to believe your Jesus-given identity above your experiences. Both cannot be right if your experience contradicts the identity Jesus gave you. Are

---

[13] The *Mirror Bible* is a paraphrased version of the Bible authored by Francios du Toit, a Messianic rabbi.

you going to believe Jesus or your experiences? Proverbs 23:7 (AMP) says,

> For as he thinks in his heart, so is he.

This is an invitation to think about yourself the way God thinks about you. You may still fall short sometimes, but you get to repent and keep pressing toward the Father.[14] To align your words, your heart, and your attitude with your new identity in Christ is to align yourself with the highest truth that you can live in. Inversely, thinking less of yourself than who God sees you as (redeemed, righteous, made new, etc.) is choosing to live by a lesser truth. Allow yourself to throw off the shackles of believing that your next screwup is imminent and start believing that the identity Christ died for is there for you to step into. No sin, shame, guilt, or condemnation can nullify what Jesus accomplished on the cross. You, on the other hand, can reject His gift and deny His power. You get to choose who you will serve. If you have made Jesus your Lord, then your fallen nature died with Christ; let it be dead.

Self-Consciousness

Self-consciousness takes your focus off Jesus and places it on yourself. Let's say you were captured by foreigners and held captive in a remote jungle. Now let's say someone skilled in navigating the jungle rescues you from your captivity. As you make your escape through the jungle, what is going to be more effective for getting out alive and free, looking at your hungry belly or keeping your eyes on your rescuer? The point is this: You can't save yourself from the sin you have committed. Jesus has to save you. If you constantly look at yourself through *your* vantage point, you'll always have a limited view. It will be limited to your own experiences. A subtle lie has permeated the thoughts of many inside and outside the church: self-consciousness, self-observation, and self-care will lead me to the truth about who I

---

[14] Proverbs 24:16–18

am. Unfortunately, this is not true. It will only lead you to believe the mess you are living in is the real you.

Now aside from the gift of new life in Christ, it is true. We are hopeless messes without Jesus. The crux of this problem is that when you consistently navel-gaze the object of your focus and attention is still you. It's a deceptive form of self-centeredness. You might even be looking at yourself, thinking about your own selfishness and ways to be more selfless. This sounds noble; however, if your personal spiritual, emotional, relational, or physical progress is always at the forefront of your mind, then your focus is still centered around you.

We are not suggesting that you don't examine your heart. We are saying that it is more effective to think about the Lord and allow Him to make the changes in your heart. Instead of praying, "Lord, help me stop being selfish, hot-tempered, frustrated, annoyed, etc.," pray, "Lord, thank You that You make all things new in me. Thank You that as I follow You, I am becoming more like You, and You are helping me. Thank You that I am getting better at thinking of others first. Thank You for making me slow to anger. Thank You for satisfying me. Thank You that I have been formed by Your love and bear the fruit of patience in my life."

Do you hear the difference? In the first statement, you are putting the focus on you and your shortcomings. In the following statements, you are praising the Lord for what He has already done and retraining your mind and heart to have His thoughts about you.

Death and life are in the power of the tongue.
(Proverbs 18:21 ESV)

Retraining our thoughts and prayers dramatically changed our personal thought lives *and* our circumstances. Now we thank the Lord for what is true from heaven's perspective about ourselves, our marriage, our friends, our finances, etc. This simple adjustment has shifted our prayers and thoughts from all the things that were lacking to what God has said about ourselves, others, and circumstances. We started to see the positive changes manifest sooner than expected, and we would encourage you to make this adjustment in the things you say and pray for.

Offense

> A brother offended is more unyielding than a
> strong city, and quarreling is like the bars of a
> castle. (Proverbs 18:19 ESV)

Taking offense is somehow encouraged in our society. How many times have you heard the phrase, "I'd give them a piece of my mind" or "I can't believe he said *that* to you!" Annoyance, frustration, and jealousy are commonly accepted emotions, so long as they are not held against us. These attitudes toward people or life's circumstances are some of the most counterproductive feelings that we can allow into our lives. Proverbs 18:19 says that being offended by someone builds walls or strongholds in your life. Strongholds and walls are things meant to keep people out. Although this may sound like a good thing, walls and bars also keep people in. Living with offense doesn't free you; it keeps you bound to the offender.

Choosing to live an unoffendable life feels like a great injustice. After all, that jerk who cut you off shouldn't be let off so easily. Maybe it was the kid who didn't show you the respect you deserved in front of your friends, or the barista who gave you the wrong drink in the drive-through, and you were already running late. We have an innate cry for justice that wants to call people to account for their mistakes against us. To continually walk in forgiveness can almost seem impossible at times. Each day presents new opportunities to be offended. In a culture that celebrates being offended, it will be countercultural to live without offense. In fact, people might even get offended at you for your choosing not to take offense.

We have heard teachings about how Jesus lived without offense. We began reading through the Gospels with this in mind, searching for an occasion where Jesus did take offense. Offense is such a normal part of life. Surely Jesus was offended by someone at some point! We could not find an example anywhere, though we did find many examples where we would have been offended if we were in His place. Offense often results from feeling like you've been gypped, counted out, misrepresented, oppressed, or harmed in some way. How did Jesus live without offense? The phrase spoken by Jesus on the cross gives our answer. "Forgive them, Father, for they know not what they do."[15] You might hear this and want to claim that the people you are offended by acted on purpose, giving you the right to be offended. In the passage in Luke 23, it is obvious that the people crucifying Jesus did know what they were doing. They may not have known He was the Son of God, but they did know He was innocent according to the law. So how do we live without offense? By choosing a lifestyle of forgiveness.

> Repay no one evil for evil, but give thought to do what is honorable in the sight of all. If possible, so far as it depends on you, live peaceably with all. Beloved, never avenge yourselves, but leave it to the wrath of God, for it is written, "Vengeance is mine, I will repay," says the Lord. To the contrary, "if your enemy is hungry, feed him; if he is thirsty, give him something to drink; for by so doing you will heap burning coals on his head." (Romans 12:17–20 ESV)

Living a lifestyle free of offense will liberate you and those around you. You will no longer have to drag the person around who is bound to you by your offense. It's likely they did not feel the weight of your offense. Your emotional and spiritual energy will no longer be drained and will be available for pressing forward on the path of righteousness.

Inner Healing

Inner healing ministries focus on working through hurts of your past to lead you into more freedom in your future. These ministries

---

[15] Luke 23:34 ESV

are designed to assist people by working through ungodly beliefs, generational problems, and trauma that are negatively impacting their lives. All good inner healing then replaces the damaged areas with the plans of God for their lives. From our personal experience, these ministries can be wonderful tools to help navigate some of the things that hold you back and equip you with tools to move you forward. Acknowledging pain is vital to moving forward into a healthy life. However, we do encourage you to utilize these tools to press toward a victorious future and not use your past as a reason to be held back. Jesus is more than enough to heal the past, sit with you in the present, and launch you forward into a brighter future.

Damage is done when people are made aware of trauma and pain without moving past it by the power of Jesus's blood into their God-given identities. We have known many people who have gone through inner healing and claimed a change in their lives because of it. However, in conversations, they constantly refer to the trauma they experienced and relate their relational problems to the fact that their trauma has left them damaged or deficient. Certainly, there is time and process. God is kind enough not to bring everything to the surface at once, but as you journey toward your true identity, claim Jesus's righteousness and wholeness as yours! He has given it to you.

Breakthrough and Revival Defined

Breakthrough and *revival* are words that are getting a lot of attention in modern Christendom. Based on your experience and background, these words might elicit eager anticipation, or they might generate derision. For some church cultures, these are goals that people constantly pursue. Other church cultures suppress change to preserve tradition and familiarity. It is important to remember that if God is bringing about change, then it is for our benefit.

Breakthrough and revival are gifts from God. It is important to steward these encounters well. There were thousands of people who had real encounters with Jesus while He was on the earth, yet they did not allow themselves to be changed. This still happens today. Rather than be truly changed by the encounter, they leave the high the experience provided, only to revert to old behaviors when faced with conflict. Some get stuck in a cycle of looking for the so-called *mountaintop experiences* over and over again. Others just give up trying because of their personal failure to change. Still others relegate these terms to charismatic jargon and work to spread disbelief or to discredit real movements of God.

Let's define these terms in this context. *Breakthrough* is a noticeable change in someone's life that leads them to more freedom in an area in their life which previously held them captive. *Revival* is the rebirthing of someone to new life in Christ, or a new vigor, excitement, passion for their salvation, and redemption. These moments are full of potential and can catapult you to the next level in your spiritual walk. These often include encounters with God where the spiritual, emotional, and even physical realities change. They might come as divine healings, visions, words of truth spoken over you that resonate deeply within your heart, an experience of God's tangible love, or any other way that God wants to meet you. They are moments in life when God touches you and impacts the way you think, live, and behave. These moments, like Moses at the burning bush, have the potential to radically change the trajectory of your life. These moments serve as Ebenezers, or markers, where we can look back at how God has moved in the past. They are an encouragement that He has been faithful in the past and will continue to be in the future.

> Jesus Christ is the same yesterday and today and forever. (Hebrews 3:8 NIV)

> For every one of God's promises is "Yes" in him. Therefore, through him we also say "Amen" to the glory of God. (2 Corinthians 1:20 CSB)

Stewarding Breakthrough and Revival

Breakthrough and revival are beautiful times when you experience God in a way that is unexplainable and impactful. They are the experiential components that bring your theology to revelation. Here are some things to consider when it comes to encounters with God.

The spiritual realm is real.

> For we do not wrestle against flesh and blood, but against the rulers, against the authorities, against the cosmic powers over this present darkness, against the spiritual forces of evil in the heavenly places. (Ephesians 6:12 ESV)

We want to be clear that just as there are holy encounters with God, there are also demonic encounters. The holy encounters with God will align with the heart of God found in the Scriptures. They will lead to the death of the sinful man and bring life to the spiritual man inside you. The fruit of these encounters should lead you toward the things of God, the heart of God, and toward the love of God. This love of God includes His love for you and other people. It should also lead you to more freedom and understanding of your identity as a new creation in Christ. Encounters with God do not lead toward more bondage.

> Now the Lord is the Spirit, and where the Spirit of the Lord is, there is freedom. (2 Corinthians 3:17 ESV)

Demonic things can masquerade as good things initially.

> And no wonder, for even Satan disguises himself as an angel of light. So it is no surprise if his servants, also, disguise themselves as servants of righteousness. Their end will correspond to their deeds. (2 Corinthians 11:14–15 ESV)

Looking at the fruit of the encounter can give insight into the origin of it.

For no good tree bears bad fruit, nor again does
a bad tree bear good fruit, for each tree is known
by its own fruit. For figs are not gathered from
thornbushes, nor are grapes picked from a bram-
ble bush. The good person out of the good treasure of his heart produces good, and the evil person out of his evil treasure produces evil, for out
of the abundance of the heart his mouth speaks.
(Luke 6:43–45 ESV)

Moses's Encounter

Exodus 3 describes the account of Moses's encounter at the
burning bush. The burning bush was an invitation for Moses to have
a meeting with God. A strange sight caused Moses to stop and take
note amid a normal day. God likes your attention. It is always good to
be looking for ways that He might be seeking your attention. What
things are out of the ordinary, strange, or possibly even concerning in
your life? It is possible that the Lord is inviting you to an encounter
with Him. The Lord responded to Moses when he *turned aside to see*
the burning bush. The Lord will respond to you when you turn aside
and ask Him to speak. It may not be an audible voice like Moses
experienced, but if God is drawing your attention to something, then
He likely has something to say.

When Moses turned aside to the burning bush, it was his first
step to receiving what God had for him. Once God had Moses's
attention, Moses said, "Here I am." It's one thing to recognize that
God wants to get your attention, and it's another thing to come to
Him and ask for more understanding. Then Moses heard, "Don't
come any closer," which was the first command. Obedience in the
process of following God is necessary to receive all that He has for
you. Obedience is tied to love. Jesus is quoted in John 14:15 (ESV)
as saying,

If you love me, you will keep my commandments.

God will lead you in His love, but for you to reciprocate His love, you need to do what He tells you. This gentle instruction often comes in little steps. A friend of ours calls these faith-building experiences. God is good at growing what tiny seeds of faith we sow into beautiful trees where others can find protection and rest. The little steps and small growth typically come before He asks us to take the bigger steps. Luke 16:10 (ESV) reminds us,

> One who is faithful in a very little is also faithful
> in much.

Moses obeyed the commands to not come closer and to remove his sandals with a heart of humility. It was then that the Lord revealed the purpose behind the strange burning bush: the commissioning of Moses to lead Israel out of slavery. Notice that the call on Moses's life wasn't for him. His call from the Lord and his rise in leadership was for a greater call to serve others, not himself. It's important to recognize that Moses was qualified for leadership because of his willingness to be obedient and his humility. God could trust him with much because he proved to be trustworthy in little.[16] This encounter with God changed Moses's life and the course of history for the nation of Israel. Your time with God should not be diminished to getting enough encouragement to get through the day. It just might be that God has something far greater planned for your life than you are aware of. The best way to be made aware is to turn aside and seek the *Lord*. You don't need a talking bush because God gave us Holy Spirit to comfort and instruct us. Don't relegate your time to just learning more about God on an intellectual level. Seek to hear Him and know Him on a personal level. Don't settle for a relationship *to* God when you can have a relationship *with* God.

---

[16] Luke 16:10

Skeptics

Hesitation and skepticism are not unique to the twenty-first century. They are still problematic today just as they were during the dawn of the first century AD when people were skeptical about Jesus and hesitant to follow Him. It is easy to put on skepticism, and it feels safe. For those who wear it regularly, it may feel like protection or wisdom. The reality is that skepticism and hesitation often cause us to avoid pursuing things that God wants us to step into. When we avoid things which are foreign or out of our control, we limit growth.

For those who are skeptical of the moves of God, we encourage you to ask Him to open the eyes of your heart and have faith that He is trustworthy to lead you to paths of life and not destruction.[17] He is faithful to teach you what is right and navigate you through the uncharted territories of faith. You don't want to neglect the mysteries of God because these are some of the ways He uses to draw you to Himself.

> It is the glory of God to conceal things, but the glory of kings is to search things out. (Proverbs 25:2 ESV)

Don't allow fear or skepticism to dominate your walk of faith. If there are things that you don't understand, simply ask Him, "Lord, if it's of You, I want it. If it is not, I don't." God is powerful enough to protect you and the Holy Spirit is a good teacher.

> But the Helper, the Holy Spirit, whom the Father will send in my name, he will teach you all things and bring to your remembrance all that I have said to you. (John 14:26 ESV)

---

[17] Psalm 51:10, Ephesians 1:18, Proverbs 3:5

Chasers

It is a good thing to pursue the heart of God along with His presence and His glory! However, encounters with God are meant to propel you in maturity and love, not leave you endlessly chasing spiritual and emotional highs. Encounters often have actionable steps for you to exercise after the feelings wane. Walking out these actionable steps that were revealed in your encounter with the Lord brings maturity. This results in steadfast spiritual confidence and enthusiasm. An actionable step might be to reframe your thought life around certain ungodly beliefs that you're holding onto. If God reveals to you that you have a belief about yourself that is ungodly, talk to Him about it and ask Him to reveal the godly belief to replace it. Godly beliefs can also be sought out in the Scriptures with help from the Holy Spirit. You have the authority to renounce ungodly beliefs in your life through Jesus. You must always be diligent to replace them with godly beliefs. While it is good to renounce ungodly beliefs and push out lies, if you don't replace the lies with truth, then you will leave a vacancy in your life for more lies to inhabit. It is good to remind yourself of these things every time the enemy tries to make you identify with an ungodly idea.

God may also reveal unforgiveness during an encounter with Him. Unforgiveness has the potential to damage your spiritual and physical health.[18] When God reveals unforgiveness, be quick to forgive, or at the very least ask Him for help to forgive. If you keep chasing the highs to feel God but neglect to take care of the issue He reveals, such as unforgiveness, you won't grow past the need for constant personal ministry. The same issues will persist. Make room for the sword of truth and partner your faith in obedience to God's instructions to you. Truth combats the deception of the enemy and strengthens and matures your faith.

---

[18] Johns Hopkins Medicine published an article, "Forgiveness: Your Health Depends on It," which explained that unforgiveness can have a negative impact on your physical health; but forgiveness can improve heart health, sleep, cholesterol, pain, blood pressure, anxiety, depression, and stress.

More often than not, God isn't showing us something wrong with us in encounters with Him. God loves to tell us how much He loves us. Don't be caught off guard if you consistently receive encouragement from Him. Receive the encouragement and apply it to your identity. Knowing who you are according to God is more powerful than we realize. Romans 1:6 in the *Mirror Bible* says, "In Jesus, you individually discover who you are." It also says in James 1:2, "Your joy in who you know you are leads you out triumphantly [over temptation] every time."

Becoming firmly rooted in your new identity is the second key to unlocking the kingdom life. Your new God-given identity frees you from the heaviness of the world and enables you to approach your relationship with God boldly.

> Let us then with confidence draw near to the throne of grace, that we may receive mercy and find grace to help in time of need. (Hebrew 4:16 ESV)

INTIMACY

> But seek first the kingdom of God and his righ-
> teousness, and all these things will be added to
> you.
>
> —Matthew 6:33 (ESV)

Now that we have established some context for your faith through a deepened understanding of Israel and your new identity, intimacy is a good next step for growing faith. Intimacy has the ability to take you beyond Jesus being just your Savior and make Him your Lord. Intimacy is cultivated where theology meets revelation. Revelation is obtained through encounters with God. Far too often, people are taught theology in the Bible, but they haven't allowed enough space for encounters. God uses encounters to pull knowledge from people's heads down into their hearts. This exchange of knowledge going from head to heart is the very thing that will transform and lead you to greater intimacy with God. Your heart needs to be ignited by the truth. If you are content to settle for good theology without revelation, then your heart and life will lack power and victory. On the flip side, if you are passionate and on fire but lack good theology, then you are likely to go out strong only to stumble hard or hit a wall.

It was once described to us that a good Christian is like a fast-moving freight train on a straight track. The teaching related good theology to mass, and related passion to velocity. People with good theology and no passion have a lot of mass, but move very slowly, if at all. If they run into a barrier, it will stop them. Their lack of passion (or velocity) means they don't have enough momentum to blow through the wall. People who are very passionate without good theology will probably be moving very quickly, but when they hit a wall, they will just bounce off of it. Their lack of good theology (or mass) means they also lack momentum. However, if the two are coupled, the result is similar to Newton's second law of motion: mass times velocity equals momentum. People who are full of good theology and also full of passion will blow through any barrier they encounter because they carry so much momentum.

Holy Spirit is the third person of the trinity who lives inside you and carries the power of God.

> If the Spirit of Him who raised Jesus from the dead dwells in you, He who raised Christ Jesus from the dead will also give life to your mortal bodies through His Spirit who dwells in you. (Romans 8:11 ESV)

Having a deep and living relationship with Holy Spirit will radically change your life. Holy Spirit is personal, specific, and fully able to communicate love to you and through you. He will give you guidance when guidance is needed and comfort when comfort is needed. Making time for intimacy with God will lead you to a deeper understanding of who you are and what your calling is.

Goodness of God

To have true intimacy with God, you must believe He is good. Because there is no one on earth who is infinitely good; it is difficult to imagine having such a perfect God. Yet, having a deep revelation that God is for you, wants to bless you, and celebrates having a relationship with you is pivotal to living out radical faith.

> Let us then with confidence draw near to the
> throne of grace, that we may receive mercy and
> find grace to help in time of need. (Hebrews 4:16
> ESV)

He is not a God who is trying to teach us lessons through hardship, although "we know that for those who love God all things work together for good, for those who are called according to his purpose" (Romans 8:28 ESV). Rather, "The thief comes only to steal and kill and destroy, but [Jesus] came that they may have life and have it abundantly" (John 10:10, ESV). God's infinite goodness toward you, and His deep love for you, is the framework to see all things in life with Him.

Faith

For many, faith is a lofty and obscure idea with little practical application. It can feel so allusive.

> And without faith it is impossible to please
> Him, for whoever would draw near to God must
> believe that He exists and that He rewards those
> who seek Him. (Hebrews 11:6 ESV)

Therefore, it is good that we press a little further to discover what faith really is.

> Now faith is the *substance* of things hoped for, the
> evidence of things not seen. (Hebrews 11:1 KJV,
> emphasis ours)

This means that faith has a concreteness or tangibility to it. When living a kingdom life, faith is the solid foundation that stands in the gap between what we know in God and what we see. Faith is the *choice* of the heart to believe against the all-natural understanding that God is willing and capable to do what He has promised. This means there will be times in a life of faith where what is experienced or seen in the natural realm will seemingly contradict what is being perceived in the spiritual realm. "So we fix our eyes not on what is seen, but on what is unseen, since what is seen is temporary, but what is unseen is eternal" (2 Corinthians 4:18 NIV). Faith glorifies God because it magnifies His willingness and capability to fulfill His Word. Abraham's faith was described in Romans 4:17–22 (CSB), stating:

> In the presence of the God in whom he believed, the one who gives life to the dead and calls things into existence that do not exist. He believed, hoping against hope… He did not weaken in faith…He did not waver in unbelief at God's promise but was strengthened in his faith and gave glory to God, because he was fully convinced that what God had promised, he was also able to do. Therefore, it was credited to him for righteousness.

This passage states that Abraham was "fully convinced." The familiar passage in Mark 11:22 is typically translated as that we are to "have faith in God." The author of the *Mirror Bible*, Francois du Toit, states that it should be translated as "Have the faith of God." This implies that we are to have the same beliefs about our situations as God has about our situations! This was super helpful for us when applying faith in our lives. We no longer have to figure out what faith is through some mental exercise or spiritual gymnastics. We can base our lives and our choices on the word of God and replace our beliefs on any given topic with the beliefs of God Himself.

Prayer

Prayer is the ongoing dialogue between you and God. It is a conversation where you take time to listen. True prayer aligns your heart with God's heart, enabling you to see from heaven's perspective. It is not a list of complaints, but rather, it is the pouring out of your heart to the Father, knowing He hears you and answers you.[19] Prayer is where God reveals His character, illuminates His Scriptures, and guides your decisions. It's where a heart of stone is transformed into a heart of flesh.[20] Prayer is also a battle strategy. In prayer, you can rebuke the enemy, replace lies with truth, and speak things into being.[21] It's in the continual communication with God that you can present your requests to Him or declare war on the enemy's attacks.[22]

Through prayer, a relationship with God is cultivated so that you can hear His voice more clearly.[23] The Holy Spirit speaks through the written Word of God, the Bible (*logos*), and personal (*rhema*) words to you. The Greek term *rhema* is found in the Scriptures and describes the words that Holy Spirit speaks individually and specifically to your life. Personal *rhema* words will always align with the character and nature of God found in the Scriptures, but they will not necessarily quote a Scripture.

> So faith comes from hearing, and hearing through
> the word *(rhema)* of Christ. (Romans 10:17 ESV)

If you find yourself struggling with this idea, it might be helpful to note that the righteous men and women led by God in the Old Testament, before the Torah was written, heard God's voice for themselves personally. In other words, before the Bible, the Word of God, could be *logos*, it had to be *rhema*.

Baptism of the Holy Spirit

Speaking in tongues, or a personal prayer language, is evidence of being baptized by the Holy Spirit. Although the Holy Spirit indwells every person who calls on Jesus to be their Savior, being

---

[19] Jeremiah 29:12, James 1:5, Psalm 91:15
[20] Ezekiel 36:26
[21] Romans 4:17
[22] Matthew 4
[23] John 10:47

baptized in the Holy Spirit equips a Christian to walk in a deeper relationship with greater power, wisdom, and revelation along with the gift of God to pray in an unknown language where Holy Spirit prays through your mouth.

> For one who speaks in a tongue speaks not to men but to God; for no one understands him, but he utters mysteries in the Spirit. (1 Corinthians 14:2 ESV)

Have you ever not known what to pray? Or the pain of a circumstance was almost too much to utter words? Or maybe the joy in something was too great to express in English. Praying in the Holy Spirit allows your heart to cry out to the Lord and your mind does not have to think of the right words.

> If I pray in a different language, my spirit is praying, but my mind does nothing. (1 Corinthians 14:14 NCV)

It can be a great relief to know that your heart can communicate with God even if you can't articulate all you want to say.

Healing

The topic of healing has the capacity to derail people's faith and stir up strife and confusion in the church. For us, this teaching was highly offensive when we first wrestled with the meaning and implication of these Scriptures. However, it is difficult to read through the New Testament and disregard Jesus's commands to "heal the sick, raise the dead, cleanse those who have leprosy, drive out demons. Freely you have received; freely give" (Matthew 10:8 NIV). Additionally,

> And the prayer of faith will save the one who is sick, and the Lord will raise him up. And if he has

committed sins, he will be forgiven. Therefore,
confess your sins to one another and pray for one
another, that you may be healed. The prayer of a
righteous person has great power as it is working.
(James 5:15–16 ESV)

These passages can be challenging, especially if you have testimonies of people not being healed despite your diligent prayers. It's in this that you must humble yourself and not let experience alone be your teacher but stand on the words of God in the Bible. The Lord does not send you out on missions doomed for failure or ask you to do something that He won't equip you for. If He has commissioned you to pray for the sick, you must determine that it is His will to heal. Many people grow weary, frustrated, or even lose faith in God because of their disappointment when prayers seem to be left unanswered. If your experiences don't match what Jesus teaches in the Bible, then it is an opportunity to press into the heart of God where He will teach you and grow you. Don't let an experience of failure be your teacher. Allow the One who set the standard to equip and empower you to do it.

Fasting

Jesus follows His instruction on how to pray in Matthew 6 with the statement, "And when you fast." This implies an expectation that His followers will fast. Fasting is a natural extension of prayer. Fasting isn't a way to manipulate God to answer prayers more quickly, or on your terms. Rather, in denying fleshly desires, you are more able to attentively hear and follow Holy Spirit's leading. A lifestyle of fasting is a way to quiet the noise that can clutter your mind and heart and regain clarity in hearing God's voice.

Fasting is also a very effective way to eliminate unbelief. Unbelief gains its hold in the mind and blocks faith. Jesus teaches that it is the component of faith in a prayer that gives it power to affect change. When we fast, we are actively suppressing our mind's impulse to eat or to participate in something we enjoy. This exercise of suppression strengthens the Holy Spirit's control over our flesh, giving room for the faith of God to dominate our thoughts. In Matthew 17, the disciples asked Him why they couldn't deliver a demon from a boy. Jesus replied that it was because of their unbelief. He then goes on to say, without changing the subject, that this kind (of unbelief) only comes out through prayer and fasting.

Incorporating fasting into your life does not have to be overly complicated. The point of fasting is to suppress the flesh by withholding something that the flesh likes. Some people start out fasting one meal a day; others might fast everything but water for twelve or perhaps twenty-four hours. Others might give up a favorite food or beverage for a week or a month. Our recommendation is that if fasting is not familiar to you, then start small and ask God for one thing to fast for a day. It is also important to replace whatever you are fasting with prayer. Fasting alone might effectively suppress the flesh, but it is the component of prayer that helps us align our thoughts and beliefs with the Lord's thoughts and beliefs.

Water Baptism

Being baptized in water is the outward expression of the inward decision to follow Jesus and make Him your Savior. Baptism is a depiction of your spiritual death and resurrection, just as Jesus died and rose again. When you make Jesus your Lord, you die to your old life and are raised to a new life in Him.

> Now if we have died with Christ, we believe that we will also live with him. We know that Christ, being raised from the dead, will never die again; death no longer has dominion over him. For the death he died he died to sin, once for all, but the life he lives he lives to God. So you also must consider yourselves dead to sin and alive to God in Christ Jesus. (Romans 8:8–11 ESV)

Studying the Bible

The Bible is a love letter from God to His people. It is chocked full of promises that are available to you, but they must be believed. When your perspective of the Bible shifts from being a theological textbook to the living, breathing Word of God to you personally, it will ignite your heart to receive the love of God in new ways. The overarching narrative of the Bible is a good God who wants to be involved in the lives of His people. This is the lens in which to study it. The New Testament is the fulfillment of the Old Testament's prophecies for the long-awaited Messiah. The New Testament records the very Words of Jesus and describes the church that formed after His ministry, death, and resurrection. Studying the Bible enables us to see the consistency of God's goodness, love, and faithfulness toward His people. It teaches us who the God we serve is.

Just as it is important to spend time listening to the *rhema*, or freshly spoken Word of God, it is also important to spend time in the *logos*, or written Word of God. Studying and thinking about what the Bible says and teaches will assist you in cultivating a profound intimacy with your Creator. He can and will meet you both in the Holy Scriptures and in the quiet place. He will use both to tell you how much He loves you and to strengthen your connection to Him.

We have now unpacked the significance of Israel, the newness of your redeemed identity, and ways to pursue intimacy with God. We will now explore the final key to unlocking a kingdom life. We call this key *industry*.

INDUSTRY

Industry is the fourth key to unlocking a kingdom life. It is the natural outcome of accepting the Gospel, walking in your new identity, and cultivating intimacy with God. Industry, in this context, describes doing the work of God's holy people. Aligning our hearts with the priorities of God ensures that we don't labor in vain for a life of selfishness but live the life He has called us to. The Bible gives insight into the responsibilities and tasks of believers. It also highlights the callings and giftings of believers to equip the church to fulfill its role on the earth. We will first look at the Great Commission and then run through the giftings God gave His people to carry out this commission.

The Great Commission

> And Jesus came and said to them, "All authority in heaven and on earth has been given to Me. Go therefore and make disciples of all nations, baptizing them in the name of the Father and of the Son and of the Holy Spirit, teaching them to observe all that I have commanded you. And behold, I am with you always, to the end of the age." (Matthew 28:18–20 ESV)

This passage highlights the calling of believers to share their faith with the world. Sharing your faith can look many different ways. It might be talking to your neighbor about what Jesus has done in your life or serving in a local or global ministry. Considering

Jesus's life and ministry, it is obvious that He prioritized loving and serving people while remaining pure in faith.

> Religion that is pure and undefiled before God
> the Father is this: to visit orphans and widows
> in their affliction, and to keep oneself unstained
> from the world. (James 1:27 ESV)

Living out your faith can also look like entering society to bring heaven's ideas to earth in different parts of life. As Jesus prayed in Matthew 6:10 (ESV), "Your kingdom come, your will be done, on earth as it is in heaven," it is part of the call of the believer to participate in creating governments, economies, families, education, and entertainment that align with the kingdom of heaven.[24] This is not about dominating these areas of society in a forceful or oppressive way. Rather, it is about believers carrying life, beauty, and wholeness into areas of society where darkness has previously prevailed.

> The earth is the Lord's, and everything in it, the
> world, and all who live in it. (Psalm 24:1 NIV)

Therefore we can go with confidence into the secular world knowing that all the earth was created by God and for God. To restore things back to their fullest and most beautiful design is to magnify God in a tangible way.

---

[24] It is difficult to determine where this concept originated; however, the teaching of going into different areas of society with kingdom purpose and perspective has been taught and elaborated by many leaders including Loren Cunningham, Lance Wallnau, and Johnny Enlow to name a few.

Spiritual Gifts and Callings

Spiritual gifts are given by God to unify and assist the church (people of God) in their work. Although not an exhaustive list of spiritual gifts, Romans 12:6 (NLT) highlights a few:

> In his grace, God has given us different gifts for doing certain things well. So if God has given you the ability to prophesy, speak out with as much faith as God has given you. If your gift is serving others, serve them well. If you are a teacher, teach well. If your gift is to encourage others, be encouraging. If it is giving, give generously. If God has given you leadership ability, take the responsibility seriously. And if you have a gift for showing kindness to others, do it gladly.

It is important to recognize the strengths and weaknesses of yourself and others, especially when it comes to ministry in the church. People are more likely to recognize the value of their own gifts and contributions but don't always notice or honor the gifts of others with the same esteem. Conversely, people may discount their gifts and overemphasize the gifts of others. It is important to stay in your lane. Don't allow differences to cause division, but allow the differences to be a delight because where one lacks, another abounds. This celebration of differences, all unified in Christ, will propel the church to move powerfully in love the way it was intended to.

> There are different kinds of gifts, but the same Spirit distributes them. There are different kinds of service, but the same Lord. There are different kinds of working, but in all of them and in everyone it is the same God at work. (1 Corinthians 4:4–6 NIV)

The body of Christ has synergistic effectiveness when the people within it love each other and unify in the heart of the Gospel. Being careful to not let offense grow amid these differences will open the doors to God's favor on His people. This will greatly impact the world.

Leadership Gifts

In addition to spiritual gifts, there are also leadership gifts, or anointings, that can be given to believers for the equipping of the church. These leadership gifts include the roles of apostles, prophets, evangelists, pastors, and teachers. The *Classic Edition of the Amplified Bible* expounds on these gifts in Ephesian 4:11:

> And His gifts were [varied; He Himself appointed and gave men to us] some to be apostles (special messengers), some prophets (inspired preachers and expounders), some evangelists (preachers of the Gospel, traveling missionaries), some pastors (shepherds of His flock) and teachers.

These gifts are intended to work together to have a well-rounded, complete church. However, the inherent strengths of one of these leadership gifts often conflict with the strengths or weaknesses of another gift. Let's go over these gifts briefly to better understand their ministry roles. Having a better understanding can promote teamwork and honor among these differing callings and perspectives.

Apostles

People with apostolic anointing will be visionary leaders who aspire to build practical avenues for the church to bring the kingdom of God to earth. They are gifted to see big-picture ideas and creatively think of ways to grow the influence of the Gospel. However, apostles can grow frustrated with details, which can cause conflict with the teacher's gift.

Prophets

People with a prophetic anointing will be leaders who hear from God clearly and desire to be radically aligned with His message. These leaders see things in black and white and may struggle with the gentleness of the pastoral anointing. While people with a prophetic gift typically perceive God's word to them in a black-and-white manner; what seems like a clear revelation to them can seem obscure to people with other giftings. Although prophets will align with biblical principles, some teachers may struggle when working with prophets because of the obscurity of the prophetic gift.

Evangelists

People with an evangelistic anointing will be leaders who are gifted in sharing the Gospel with others. They are often outside the walls of the church building because they have a strong desire to teach, preach, and share God with the unsaved world. They can be known for intensity and love. However, evangelists might struggle with the loftiness or piety of the prophetic gift because there's no time to waste with obscurity; there are people to save!

Pastors

People with a pastoral gift are the shepherds that care for the body of Christ. They are characterized by gentleness, clarity, and kindness. Although the term "Pastor" is often used as a title in the church, not all people in this role have the pastoral anointing. In fact, many in the pulpit are actually leaders with evangelistic or teaching anointings. Pastoral leaders will emphasize the necessity of ministering to people gently, which can conflict with the visionary leadership of apostles or the bluntness of prophetic leaders.

Teachers

People with teaching anointing will excel at clarifying and studying the Scriptures. They have a unique ability to communicate complicated concepts in an understandable way. Like the prophetic gift, teachers love truth and desire for people to know what they believe and to live it out. Yet, teachers can perceive prophets to be presumptuous or audacious in light of their desire for the concreteness of scriptural study.

Unity

Unity is the currency of the supernatural. Although there are various calls, giftings, denominations, and doctrines within the global church, when the message of Jesus is the focus despite differing methodologies, God will dwell in our midst. When God dwells amid our hearts, lives, and churches, then we experience the supernatural power and abundant goodness of God at work.

> Finally, brothers and sisters, rejoice! Strive for full restoration, encourage one another, be of one mind, live in peace. And the God of love and peace will be with you. (2 Corinthians 13:11 NIV)

CONCLUDING THOUGHTS

The Gospel is overwhelmingly the best news in existence. Life in God can radically change our lives and captivate the world. The story of Israel highlights the beauty of a relationship with messy people and a good God. Jesus came through Israel, and now all people are invited to call on the Jewish God to free them from the bondage of death and the effects of sin. By allowing the magnificent goodness and love of God to redefine who you are, your interactions with Him will subsequently change. Embracing your new identity in Him leads you to have the confidence to seek after Him in deep friendship and intimacy. In this continual relationship, you allow God to fill your heart so that you may overflow with the love of God toward people.

You can't give to others what you have not yet received for yourself. Therefore to do the good works that God has set for you to do, you must allow Him to fill you. Works are empty and ineffective when they are void of love. Service to God, without the love of God, is useless. If you feel that you lack love, this is not a reprimand or excuse to not serve but rather an urging to allow the God of Heaven to love you specifically, uniquely, and perfectly. His love for you is wild! It is not weak or timid but strong and capable of carrying all of you. The good parts and the hard parts. He is available to you today. Come away with Him so that He may transform you and use you to set the world ablaze.

ABOUT THE AUTHORS

Jedediah and Tiffany Drenth are a power-packed husband-and-wife team. They desire to encourage and equip the body of Christ to be transformed into their new identities in Jesus. Jed excels at encouraging believers by promoting a loving and healthy community. Tiffany boldly lives to see people exchange lies for truth, knowing truth brings freedom. Together, they are a dynamic couple who seek to honor God with their whole lives and encourage others to do the same. They currently live in Texas with their two children and two dogs.